Dear Pat - We would like to
share with you a little slice of
'our world' on Sydney's Central
Coast - a place where we have
found much happiness & contentment
With fondness
            Deirdre & Ray.

                                    August '96.

FROM FOREST TO SEA

Sensational panoramic views of the Scenic Central Coast

This book is dedicated to my beautiful daughter, Jessica Anne.
I thank God for the miracle you are.

▲ Brisbane Water, Saratoga.
Previous page – Red Gum Forest, North Entrance.

THANK YOU

I would like to offer my sincere thanks to the sponsors who have endorsed this project and assisted and supported the production of this book.

Special thanks must go to my great staff for their hard work and perseverance. Thanks also to Ed Manners for convincing me to produce this book. And last, but most of all, to my wife Pamela, my best friend.

The
Scenic
Central Coast

To The Central Coast Tourist Board and all it's Members, thank you for your support.

WYONG SHIRE *it's a great place!*

Thank you Wyong Council for catching the vision of this book to bring it to fruition.

INTRODUCTION

Welcome to my home - an area known as the Scenic Central Coast. To me it is one of the most beautiful havens throughout Australia and through this book I hope to share it with you.

The northern boundary of the region is Frazer Park, a fantastic recreational area with miles of pristine beaches and invigorating bush walks. The Hawkesbury River to the south acts as a protective moat which has helped to keep the Central Coast unique in character. In the west the district is hedged by forests and farms with architectural reminders of our pioneering forefathers in quaint little towns like St. Albans. The Tasman Sea forms the eastern border with some of the most spectacular coastline Australia has to offer.

The 'Scenic' Central Coast - so named for the natural beauty it boasts. Idyllic beaches, diverse waterways, trickling creeks, cascading falls, abundant forests with pockets of lush rainforest, all adorn our coastal retreat. This sanctuary provides a life style second to none throughout Australia and only an hour north of Sydney.

I hope that in documenting this area I will encourage others to come and enjoy the uniqueness of the Scenic Central Coast - from Forest to Sea.

◀ Rounding up the horses, Glenworth Valley, Peats Ridge.

Horsfield Bay, Woy Woy.

Previous page – Aerial view of Wamberal and Terrigal.

Settlers Arms Inn, St Albans.

By the word of the Lord were the heavens made, and all their host by the breath of His mouth. He gathers the waters of the sea as in a bottle; He puts the deep in storage places. Let all the earth revere and worship the Lord; let all the inhabitants of the world stand in awe of Him. For he spoke, and it was done; He commanded and it stood fast.

Psalm 33: 6-9

Previous page – Somersby Falls.
Overleaf – George and Elizabeth, Macadamia Nut Farm,
         Yarramalong Valley.
Little Bumpy, Frazer Beach, Munmorah State Recreation Area. ▶
Rainforest, Central Coast. ▼

Fisherman, Forresters Beach.

Previous page – Aerial view of Woy Woy.

Pearl Beach from Mt Ettalong Lookout.

People often say to me "show me God if you think he is real". My reply is to suggest they open their eyes and look around them. It is a tragic mistake to think that the awesome complexities of creation happened by accident. As a photographer, I am forced to look at things very closely and finally I could no longer escape the reality of a designer far greater than man.

How majestic is the handiwork of the Lord, and who are we that He is mindful of us. In the glory of His creation His face can be seen and on the whisper of the wind he calls our names.

Previous page – Fern regrowth after fire, Presidents Hill, Gosford.
Overleaf – Autumn leaves, Oak Road, Matcham.
◀ Hire boats, Tuggerah Lakes, The Entrance.
▼ Pelicans, Brisbane Water.

Saint Barnabas Church, Yarramalong, opened in 1885. The oldest church in the Wyong Shire.

Old Silo, Dooralong, built 1904 and used as silage storage for dairy cattle feed.

Wandering down the streets of Old Sydney Town is like stepping back in time to our colonial past. This faithful re-creation of the beginnings of our nation gives us an insight into what it was like to be thrust into a wild land and have to carve out a living.

We come from a hardy breed who overcame many obstacles to help make this great country what it is today. Maybe a walk through the heritage of our past, will help put into perspective, problems that sometimes come our way.

Overleaf – Reflections at Avoca Beach.
◄ Old Sydney Town, Pacific Highway, Somersby.
▼ Firing the Cannon, Old Sydney Town.

The old barn lingers on. It has weathered many storms and each one has etched a little more character into its frame.

As we drive by and see it still standing, it serves as an inspiration to us all and a reminder that despite the things that come our way, character is built as we stand firm in the face of adversity.

Previous page – Beside still waters, Terrigal Beach.
Overleaf – Sunrise in the forest, McPherson State Forest, Kulnura.
◀ The Old Barn, Wisemans Ferry Road, Mangrove Mountain.
▼ Close up of the Old Barn.

Birdie Beach, Frazer Park, Munmorah State Recreational Area.

Previous page – Fern Forest, The Ferneries, Matcham.

Maitland Bay, Bouddi National Park.

▲ Shore break, Wamberal Beach.

▲ Ferris Wheel, The Entrance.
◄ Summer Carnival, The Entrance.
Overleaf – Shooting Gallery, The Entrance.

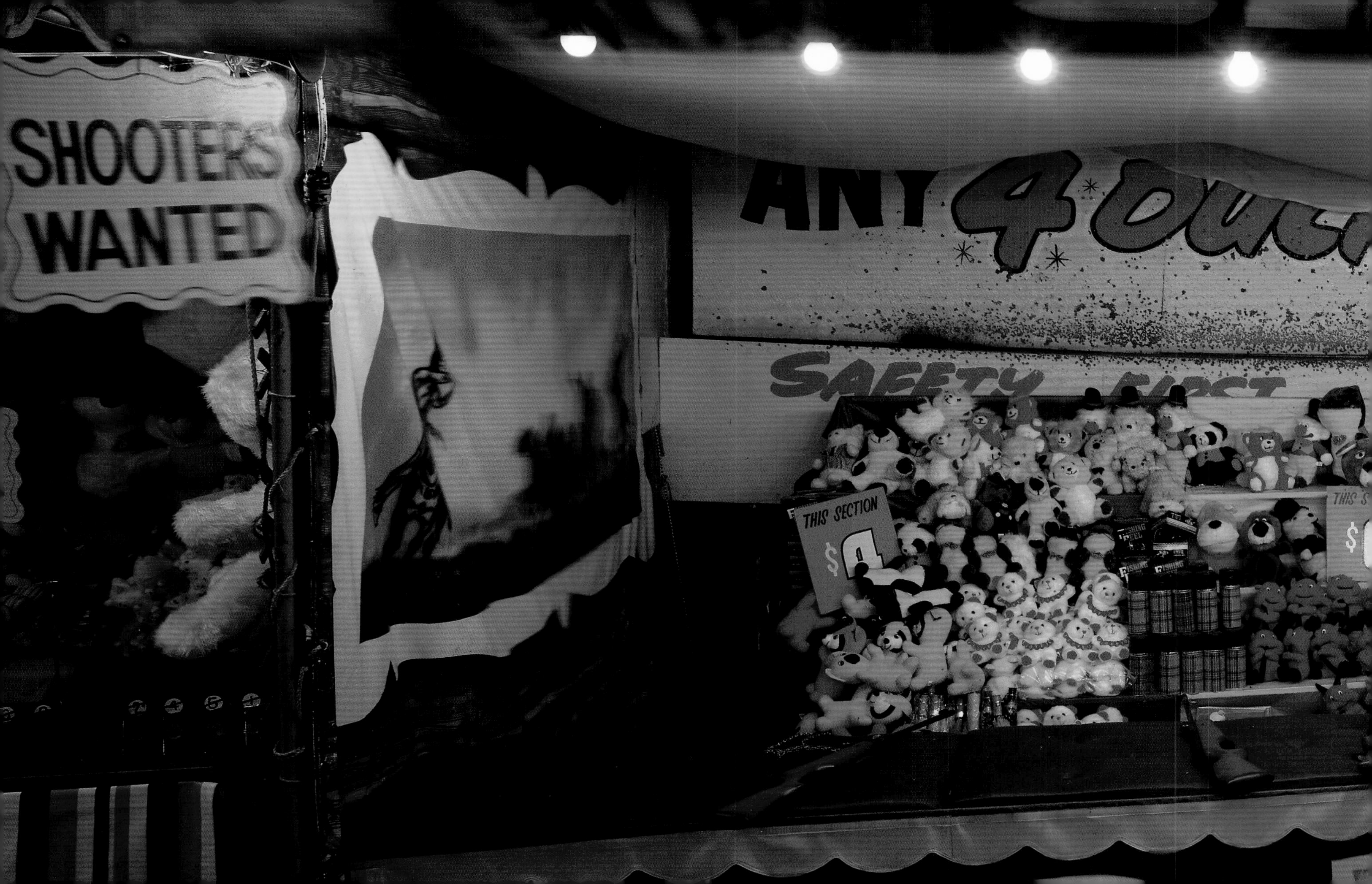
SHOOTERS
WANTED
ANY 4
THIS SECTION

The Rip Bridge, Booker Bay.

Previous page – Aerial view, Avoca Beach.

The Lady Kendall, Gosford Wharf.

Morning glow, Avoca Beach.

Pelicans feeding, The Entrance.

▲ Lightning Strike, The Haven, Terrigal.
◄ Norah Head Lighthouse, Norah Head.

Previous page – Big surf at Forresters Beach.   69

Patonga Beach and The Hawkesbury River in the background.

Previous page – Floods Creek, Somersby.

Gosford City and Brisbane Water.

78   *Previous page –* Sunrise at Soldiers Beach, Norah Head.

▲ Sunrise at Avoca Beach.

FROM FOREST TO SEA
ISBN   0 646 14847 8
Pictures and text: Ken Duncan
© **Ken Duncan**
First published in 1993 by Ken Duncan Panographs ® Pty Limited
P.O. Box 15, Wamberal NSW 2260 Australia. Phone: 61-43-67 6777
1st reprint 1994, 2nd reprint 1996.
This edition printed in Hong Kong by South China Printing Co. Ltd.

Previous – Foot Bridge, Budgewoi Creek, Budgewoi.

▼ Sunrise, Terrigal Beach.

For Thine is the Kingdom, the Power and the Glory, forever and ever, Amen.

Signed Photographic Prints of images in this book are available from Ken Duncan Australia Wide Gallery, Phone: 61-43-67 6777.